T0195956

THE ULTIMATE BOOK OF
CHORAL WARM-UPS
AND ENERGISERS
TURBO CHARGE YOUR CHOIR

Tina Reibl

authorHOUSE®

AuthorHouse™ UK
1663 Liberty Drive
Bloomington, IN 47403 USA
www.authorhouse.co.uk
Phone: 0800 047 8203 (Domestic TFN)
*   +44 1908 723714 (International)*

Published by AuthorHouse 10/14/2019

ISBN: 978-1-7283-9176-2 (sc)
ISBN: 978-1-7283-9177-9 (e)

Print information available on the last page.

Chapter title images are designed by Freepik.com

This book is printed on acid-free paper.

Contents

"Warming up and warming down is worth a little time.

Much can be accomplished with some rhythm and some rhyme.

They will help your voice to get itself to maxi-range.

Even though the sounds of each may be a little strange!"

Unknown

Introduction

Choral singing has seen a great revival with people of all ages and walks of life enjoying the pleasure of singing a wide range of repertoire in Community Choirs, Choral Societies, Gospel Choirs, Barbershop groups and Rock Choirs, to name just a few.

As each athlete performs a series of stretches and warm-ups before running a marathon, so should the choral singer warm up before leaping into the repertoire.

The Italian Bel Canto Master Giovanni Battista Lamperti is quoted as saying that:

> *"All that a singer need know could be written on the palm of my hand. Fundamentals are three: control of powerful breath energy, trueness and ease of all tones and distinct, correct diction"*

There are many wonderful books available that teach the *'trueness and ease of all tones'*, e.g. vocal technique - a list of which can be found in the appendix. However, little has been published about good breathing exercises for the choir and how to achieve *'distinct, correct diction'*.

This book aims to close the gap with a whole host of exercises to start any choir practice in a fun and engaging way!

The exercises will warm up the body, mind and voice (see Figure 1), starting with physical exercises that aim to get rid of tension and prepare the body for singing.

This will then be followed by breathing exercises that will help increase lung capacity and support sustained sound.

Finally there is a multitude of tongue twisters, nonsense poems and quodlibets (a light-hearted medley of well-known tunes) will strengthen articulation and assist with vocal blend.

All the exercises can be mixed as required using one exercise from each section.

As time is often tight, it is hard not to feel pressure to move quickly into the much needed repertoire rehearsal period, however, using these exercises will create a choir that is wide awake, alert, in a good mood and ready to work with concentration and focus. They will sing with excellent breath control, resonance and crisp diction.

THE WARM-UP PROCESS

The body is the singers' instrument and – like every other instrument, it needs to be prepared for use. A musician will unpack his instrument, set and tune it up, maybe fix a new reed to the mouthpiece, or plug it into an amplifier and adjust sound levels.

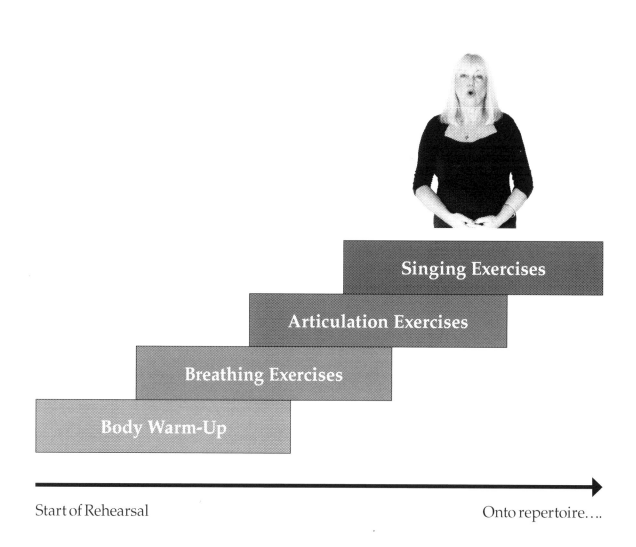

Start of Rehearsal   Onto repertoire….

CHAPTER 1

BODY WARM UP

PRINCIPLES

Choral singers will come from their ordinary working day into the rehearsal room and immediately need to switch into performance mode. Their bodies and minds need to be fit for singing, tense muscles need to relax and busy minds need to refocus. To facilitate this, the body warm-up starts with a gentle stretching of muscles to re-adjust and align the body to allow a free flow of energy and sound.

This is followed by any exercise that will wake up the right side of the brain, where rhythm and rhyme reside, to bring the whole choir into focus and help with physical coordination and creativity.

THE EXERCISES

Simple Stretches

1. Stand with your feet shoulder width apart, toes pointing forwards, and imagine that you have a string attached to the top of your head pulling you up. Slightly bend your knees and relax your arms at your side. Now repeatedly turn your torso from side to side, letting your relaxed arms swing from left to right.

2. Clench your hands into fists and swing one arm over the opposite shoulder, swing the other arm up behind your back landing both fists on your spine as close to each other as you can.

3. Interlock your fingers and turning the palms to face upwards, stretch your arms straight up over your head whilst simultaneously pushing down into your feet. Hold this stretch for a few breaths.

4. With your arms still stretched above your head, turn your torso to the right, holding as long as is comfortable, then turn to the left side.

5. Bringing your torso back to centre, take a deep breath in and let go of all the air on a 'sch' sound, bending forward from the hips and dropping down. Let your arms and head hang limp like a rag doll.

6. Breathe in very slowly as you roll upwards starting from the base of your spine and repeat exercises 5. and 6. once more. Finish exercise with an exhale.

In Bloom

Sit in your chair, feet firmly rooted on the ground, back straight and sitting on the front of the chair. Lengthen your back. Put both hands on your chest and imagine you are a flower bud, ready to blossom.

Raise your arms over your head whilst inhaling and rest in full bloom for a moment. Come back to being a flower bud and repeat.

Morning Ride

Remain seated and pretend you are riding a horse. Settle into your imaginary saddle, take the reins, put your feet into the stirrups and start riding! Wave to passers-by, use your whip, then pull back and relax.

Stand up, roll your shoulders forwards and back, roll your head, swing your arm forwards and back.

Puppet on a String

- Stand up straight with both feet firmly grounded under your shoulders.
- Imagine little roots growing out of your feet into the ground so that you stand really solidly.
- Visualise a string attached to the top of your head pulling your spine upwards until it becomes perfectly straight.
- Pull the string a bit more until you are standing on your toes.
- Let the string also pull your facial muscles up until you are wide-eyed and smiling.
- Imagine the string being cut suddenly making you flop down from the waist.
- Allow yourself to hang limp like a rag doll for a moment.
- Letting everything hang, bounce gently from your knees coming back to your straight starting position.
- Keeping your shoulders and neck loose and relaxed, imagine a string attached
- to either side of your rib cage, holding it up after each inhalation.

Circles

With each body part mentioned below, draw four circles:

- Imagine you have a pencil attached to the tip of your nose. Draw circles onto an imaginary piece of paper on the floor in front of you, reverse the direction and draw another four circles.

- Gently roll your head in clockwise circles as large as you can, then anticlockwise.

- Draw circles in the air with your right forefinger, then with your wrist, then from your elbow and finally with your whole arm (make sure you don't hit your neighbours!) Repeat using your left forefinger, wrist, elbow and arm.

- Roll your shoulders in circles forwards, then backwards.

- Draw circles on the floor with your right foot starting small and making them bigger. Repeat with your left foot.

- Rotate your hips in circles, one way and then the other.

- Finally circle your tongue around your mouth clockwise, then anticlockwise.

Eights

Repeat each action twice:

- Imagine you have a pencil attached to the tip of your nose. Draw figure of eights onto an imaginary piece of paper on the floor in front of you. Reverse the direction.

- Draw the figure of eight with both your left and right forefingers, then from both wrists and finally from your shoulders.

- Draw a tiny figure of eight on the floor with a toe, then from the ankle and finally from the knee and hip making the figure as large as you can. Repeat with the other leg.

- Draw a figure of eight from your hips using your whole upper body

Shakes

- Shake your body!

- Smile and vigorously shake out your hands, arms, legs and feet to release tension and energise your body

- Gently shake your head

- How many ways are there to shake each limb?

- Make the movements smaller until you feel a buzzing of energy inside your body

Qi Gong

These are gentle Chinese energising and balancing exercises that should be completed slowly and mindfully. Start by imagining you are holding a ball of energy between your hands about the distance of two fists from your chest. Your elbows should be comfortably bent.

1. *Compressing the Pearl*

   Inhale moving your hands and arms out to the sides as if the ball is growing in your hands. On your exhale, compress your hands and arms back to the starting position, feeling the pressure from the imaginary ball.

2. *Opening the Chest*

   From holding the ball, start by sending your hands in a downward motion, when arms are outstretched, make and arc by swinging them out to each side up to above your head. On your exhale, reverse this motion to come back to holding your ball of energy.

3. *Holding up the Moon*

   Gently unlock your knees. Breathe in as you push your arms straight up and look up to the sky, let your palms open. Breathe out as you reverse the movement to your starting position.

4. *Swimming Dragon*

   Outstretch both arms in front of your chest with one palm facing up and the other facing down. Start to move your hands and arms in the directions your palms are facing. Smoothly turn your palms to face the opposite direction and continue moving your arms.

5. *Angry Rabbit*

   Stand on one foot and lift your arms to the side of your chest with your elbows bent. Hold the thumb and first two fingers of each hand together. At the time you change the leg you are balanced on, bring your hands together into a clap and then back to the Angry Rabbit position. You may feel like you want to do some karate

BRAIN GYM EXERCISES

It is great fun to include some basic independence 'brain gym' exercises in your warmup. These exercises balance both sides of your brain and enhance the development of neural pathways in the brain through movement.

They can bring about rapid and often dramatic improvements in focus, comprehension, communication, organisation and physical movement. They are also great for helping with memory and concentration.

Cross Walk

March on the spot bringing your knees up, raise the opposite arm to leg as you march.

Cross Crawl

Raise each knee one at a time. As you raise your right knee, touch it with your left elbow. As you raise your left knee, touch it with your right elbow.

Cross Step

Step your left foot across your right foot. Then step your right foot across your left foot.

Head & Stomach

Using one hand, tap the top of your head rhythmically. Use the other hand to rub your stomach in a circular motion. After a short while, keep your hands in their respective positions and switch their activity. You can also swap the position of your hands.

Circles

Draw circles with your right foot in a clockwise direction whilst your right hand draws circles in an anti-clockwise direction. Repeat with your left leg and hand.

Round & Square

Using your left hand or finger, draw a circle and at the same time, with your right hand or finger, draw a square.

Nose & Ear

Touch your left ear with your right hand, and place your left hand on the tip of your nose. Then touch the tip of your nose with your right hand and touch your right ear with your left hand. Repeat this as quickly as possible!

Sausage Machine

Draw circles with your right hand and let your left hand chop down vertically repeatedly. Swap hands.

Figure of Eight

Use your left hand to draw a figure of eight, and your right hand to draw a circle. Swap hands.

Lazy Eights

Using your right hand, with the thumb pointing toward the ceiling, draw three large figure of eights focussing your eyes on your thumb. Draw three more with your left hand. Then draw three more with both hands clasped together.

Foot & Arm

Make clockwise circles with both your right arm and your left foot. Repeat with your left arm and right foot. Repeat both sides making anticlockwise circles.

What's in a name?

Write your name in the air. First forwards, then backwards. Repeat with your non-dominant hand. Then use both hands together.

What a Reaction!

Learn the following actions, the numbers in brackets show the different beat counts:

Slap knees twice (1, 2)	Clap hands twice (3, 4)	Snap fingers, clap hands, snap fingers, clap hands (5, 6, 7, 8)
Touch nose with right hand and bring left hand across to touch your right ear (1, 2) Touch nose with left hand and bring right hand across to touch left ear (3, 4)	Tap your shoulders with both hands twice (5, 6)	Honk with your hands twice (7, 8)

These actions can be done to the famous 'Doodely Doo' tune by Art Kassel and Mel Stitzel - give it a go!

Now do the whole thing in double time!

Numbers

First time tap each of the following body parts eight times. Repeat the sequence tapping each body part four times, then two times and finally one time.

Start slowly and increase the speed of your tapping...

- Head
- Shoulders
- Hips
- Knees
- Toes (if you can!)

Funky Chicken

Shake each of the following body parts eight times. Repeat the sequence sharing each body part four times, then two times and finally one time.

At the end flap your wings and shout 'Funky Chicken!'

- Left foot
- Right foot
- Left arm
- Right arm
- Whole body 'hula hoop'

Enthusiasm

Word	Alive	Alert	Awake	Enthusiastic
Action:	Touch head with both hands	Touch shoulders with both hands	Touch hips with both hands	Touch knees with both hands and clap twice

Now sing and act out the Enthusiasm song!

I'm a - live, a-lert, a-wake, en-thu si - as-tic   I'm a - live, a-lert, a- wake, en-thu si - as-tic   I'm a

live, a-lert, a-wake, I'm a-wake, a-lert, a-live   I'm a - live, a-lert, a-wake, en-thu si - as - tic!

CLAPPING AND ACTION GAMES

Wake Up Clap Tap

- Leader starts by clapping slowly asking the choir to join in and follow what they do
- Change tempo of clapping e.g. faster or slower
- Change dynamics of clapping e.g. loud, soft, using just the fingertips, hollow hands etc.
- Miss out a beat and make sure the choir is paying attention and follows you
- Using your fingers gently tap your head and around your face
- Tap up along the outside of each arm and then down the inside
- Tap down along the outside of each leg to the feet
- Turn to one side and gently tap the back of the person in front of you and then change direction (for the choir leader this will most likely be an imaginary person!)
- Finish by opening your mouth to an 'ooooo' shape and tapping your cheeks

Cheerleader Clap

- Clap to the right, clap to the left
- Clap high to the right, clap high to the left
- Clap down to the right, clap down to the left

Double Double This That

Teach the choir the following actions:

Word:	"Double"	"This"	"That"
Action:	Slap knees/thighs	Clap hands together	Clap back of hands together

Now rhythmically say the following and add the actions:

Double double this this,
Double double that that,
Double this, double that,
Double double this that

Double this this,
Double that that,
Double this that,
Double double this

Double this that this,
Double that this that,
Double this this that,
Double that that this

You can also create your own variations to keep the choir on their toes:

Clapping Round

Teach the choir the following actions, the numbers in brackets show the different beats counts:

- Slap knees once, clap hands once, click fingers once, rest (1, 2, 3, 4)
- Slap knees once, clap hands once, click fingers once, rest (5, 6, 7, 8)
- Slap knees, clap hands, click fingers, clap hands, slap knees, clap hands, click fingers, rest (1, 2, 3, 4, 5, 6, 7, 8)
- Tap knees right, left right, left, right left (1-and, 2-and, 3, 4)
- Clap hands, click fingers, clap hands, rest (5, 6, 7, 8)
- Slap knees, clap hands, click fingers, clap hands, slap knees, clap hands, click fingers, rest (1, 2, 3, 4, 5, 6, 7, 8)

This little rhyme can help to memorise the actions:

Fish & chips, fish & chips,
Mushy peas with fish & chips
Vinegar with our fish & chips,
Mushy peas with fish & chips

When the choir is confident in doing the actions you can do it as a round with either two groups - second group enters when first group gets to line three of the rhyme, or four groups - each new group enters at each new line of the rhyme.

Bim Bum - Hand Clapping Song

Teach the choir the following actions:

Word:	"Bim"	"Bum"	"Biddy"
Action:	Clap hands	Snap fingers	Slap knees/thighs

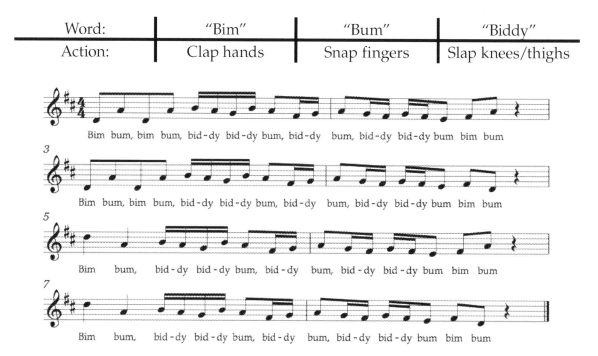

Dum, Dum, Da, Da

This is a fun tune and there are countless variations on actions that you can do with it. Here are seven different versions to try - maybe you and your choir will create your own, perhaps using the latest dance craze in the charts?

It works well if you teach the actions first and then introduce the tune.

Variation 1: Double Criss Cross

- Path both knees twice
- Cross right hand to pat left shoulder twice
- Pat both knees twice
- Cross left hand to pat right shoulder twice

Variation 2: Single Criss Cross

- Pat both knees once
- Cross right hand to pat left shoulder once
- Pat both knees once
- Cross left hand to pat right shoulder once
- Pat both knees once then cross and uncross your arms and snap your fingers

Variation 3: Hello Neighbour!

- Pat both knees twice
- Pat your right neighbour's back twice
- Pat both knees twice
- Pat your left neighbour's back twice

Variation 4: Egyptian Queen

Perform the actions as in the photos, switiching from one side to the other

Variation 5: Bodybuilder

- Clench your hands into fists
- Point both fists forward towards your knees
- Then lift to your shoulders
- Next show your biceps, alternating first with your right arm up then left

Variation 6: Hand Jive

- Pat thighs twice
- Clap hands twice
- Scissor palms twice right over left and twice left over right
- Hit right fist on top of left fist twice and left fist on top of right fist twice
- Hitch hike backwards with right thumb twice and then left thumb twice

Variation 7: The Macarena

Follow the moves in the pictures below!

- Outstretch right arm, then left (with palms down)

- Turn over right palm, turn over left palm

- Cross right palm to left shoulder, cross left palm to right shoulder

- Move right palm to back of right side of head, move left palm to back of left side of head

- Cross right palm to left hip, cross left palm to right hip

- Move right palm to right hip, move left palm to left hip

- Move right palm to right bottom cheek, move left palm to left bottom cheek

- Rock from left to right with a wiggle gyrating those hips!

The Shark Song

The leader starts saying the words and performing the actions, the choir joins in as soon as they have grasped what to do. Each verse has a different character or event **(replace words in bold)** and action that goes with it.

Words:	Actions:
Baby Shark	Use one hand for mouth like a puppet
Do, Be, Do, Be, Do, Be, Doo!	
Baby Shark	
Do, Be, Do, Be, Do, Be, Doo!	
Baby Shark	
Do, Be, Do, Be, Do, Be, Doo!	
Baby Shark!	
Mama Shark **(Continue pattern as above)**	Both arms outstretched to represents shark mouth
Daddy Shark	Use one arm and one leg to form the mouth
Grandma Shark	Both hands should be made into fists to represent a mouth with no teeth! Hide teeth in your mouth when singing it
Went for a swim	Breaststroke
Saw a Shark	Hands, palm together, above head like a shark fin
Swam real fast	Breaststroke again, really fast
Shark Attack!	Waving both arms above head while thrashing body back and forth
Lost an arm	Put one arm behind your back
Lost a leg	Hop to the beat
Then he ate me	Both arms make shark's mouth like Mama Shark
Happy Shark!	Arms above head like a shark fin again with an exaggerated smile on your face

WARM-UP ACTIONS SONGS

All the warm-up songs below should be practiced slowly to start with and increased in tempo with mastery.

They also work well as quodlibets, so you can layer any two or even all three on top of each other, allowing for the occasional small clash of harmony.

My Bonnie Lies Over the Ocean

Starting from a seated position, on the first word beginning with a 'B' stand up, and on the next work beginning with a 'B' sit down and so on.

Once this is mastered, add a clap on any word beginning with an 'O'.

Move Forwards, Move Backwards

The actions for this song are self-explanatory! Just follow the lyrics.

Move for wards, move back-wards, to the left and to the right Move for wards, move back-wards, to the

left and to the right Move for-wards, move back-wards, to the left and to the

right Move for - wards, move back-wards, to the left and to the right

Love Lifted Me

Starting from a seated position, on the word 'lifted' stand up and sit down again on the word 'me'.

Love lift - ed me_____ Love lift - ed me_____

When eve-ry-thing else was lost Love lift - ed me_____

CHAPTER 2

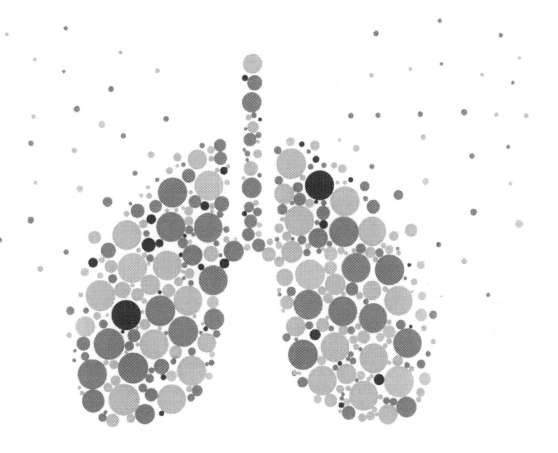

BREATHING

PRINCIPLES

Good breathing is the foundation for good singing. How you use your breath will influence the tone, volume, dynamics and the way you phrase the song. It will enable you to sustain and shape notes.

Good breathing carries many health benefits, from lowering blood pressure, improving circulation and decreasing stress. Breathing together also creates a feeling of community in the choir.

The respiration process consists of inhalation and exhalation. As you inhale the lungs fill with air and the rib cage expands outwards. The diaphragm, a dome-shaped muscle that divides the chest and abdominal area is pushed downwards.

How to inhale:
- Inhale as much air as possible in a short a time as possible
- Always inhale though your mouth, not the nose
- The inhalation should be is silent

How to exhale:
- Exhale as little air as possible – thus, maximum inhalation, minimum exhalation
- The less air you use the clearer your tone
- Sing 'on top of the breath' not 'with the breath'

How to raise your rib cage:
1. Raise your arms slowly over your head whilst inhaling fully. Hold your breath briefly and bring your arms to the sides of your rib cage to check its position. Relax your shoulders down. Exhale.
2. This time, take a short, sharp breath as if someone has surprised you and try to achieve the same elevated position of the rib cage as in the first exercise
3. Imagine you are climbing up a rope whilst you inhale. Keep pulling yourself up the rope until you have reached the top and your torso is stretched. Tie an imaginary knot in the top of your rope to keep your rib cage in this position as you breathe out.
4. Imagine a rope attached to the top of your head which goes over a pulley in the ceiling and back in front of you. Gently pull on the rope and feel your head and neck loosened as you inhale. Keep this position on the exhale.

5. Imagine you are a proud opera singer. You are holding two balloons under your armpits and someone is pumping them up as you inhale. Rest your arms in front of your these imaginary balloons.

THE EXERCISES

Breathing on a Count

- Breathe in to a count of three, hold for a count of three, exhale to a count of six
- Breathe in to a count of four, hold for a count of four, exhale to a count of eight
- Breathe in to a count of five, hold for account of five, exhale to a count of ten

Breathing on a Count (extension)

- As the exercise above, but this time whilst exhaling, pronounce *'sssss'*, then *'fffff'*, then *'sch'*

Breathing Marathon

- Breathe in together and then breathe out on *'ssss'* for as long as you can
- Repeat on *'schhh'*

You should be able to exhale for approximately 30 seconds to start with – aim to work up to minute! Or longer!

Breathing Marathon (extension)

- As the exercise above, but this time use voiced consonants *'vvvvvv'* and *'zzzzz'* as you breathe out

Follow the Leader

- Put your hands on your rib cage and breathe in, making sure that the rib cage rises and extends
- A number is called out by the choir leader. The choir breathes in for that count and exhales on *'sch'* or *'ssss'* until the lungs are completely empty.

Farinelli Breathing

- Turn your whole body a quarter to the side (so your arms don't hit your neighbour when you raise them!) Inhale to a count of eight raising your arms until they are level with your shoulders
- At the top of your inhale, roll your shoulders backwards and take a couple more short in-breaths
- Exhale on a *'zzzz'*

Alphabet

- Take a deep breath and with your hands on your rib cage, sing the alphabet in one breath

- Sing as a round with the second group starting on 'A' when the first group sing 'H'

Feather Light

- Blow a feather around the room. If you have haven't got a feather, use an imaginary one.

- Try to blow the feather really high up in the air and use a long stream of breath to get it to go up and up in the air

- Aim not to collapse your chest as you blow the feather

- Stretch your arms out to each side and imagine you have two bags of feathers hanging down from your wrists. Blow the feathers to your right, then to your left, back to your right - trying to get them to stay up in the air rather than hanging.

Balloon

- Blow up an imaginary balloon with one big breath

- Feel the tension in your abdomen increase as you keep blowing

- Take another big breath and let the air out of the balloon on a 'zzzz'

Counting on You

- Inhale deeply. Count out loud to 20 as you breathe out

- Repeat but this time count out loud to 30 as you breathe out

- How many numbers can you say in one out breath?

Even Flow

- Inhale with your hands on your rib cage. Fill up your lungs.
- Place your hand in front of your mouth as you breath out on *'ffff'*. Make sure you can feel an even flow of breath.
- Repeat on *'ssss'*

Swimming under Water

- Take a deep breath and imagine you have to swim under water for the length of a swimming pool
- Exhale your breath very slowly and evenly

Beach Ball

- Imagine you are holding a beach ball under each armpit, feel the increased breathing space as you inhale
- Exhale keeping the imaginary beach balls under your arms, feel the tension in your abdominal area increase as you exhale

Alternate nostril Breathing (This is a Pranayama yoga exercise)

- Use your right thumb to close off your right nostril
- Inhale slowly through your left nostril - pause
- Now close your left nostril with your ring finger and remove your thumb from your right nostril
- Exhale through your right nostril
- Inhale through your right nostril
- Use your thumb to close off your right nostril
- Breathe out through your left nostril and continue

Peace

- Put your fingertips together and press them gently together as you inhale
- When you have inhaled fully, stop pressing and relax with the exhale
- Imagine that you are breathing in peace and breathing out stress
- Do this twice
- On the third time, breathe in peace and breathe out peace

This exercise is brilliant for countering stage fright!

Waves

- Imagine you are breathing in through the soles of your feet
- Picture your breath as a wave going forward from your mouth, crashing at the highest notes and flooding back to you as you take another breath

Flowers and Fireworks

- Bend down to pick and imaginary flower, inhale as you come back up. Exclaim *'ah'*, *'oh'* and *'uh'* on your exhale as you appreciate the flower in your hand
- Imagine you are watching an amazing fireworks display in the sky. Exclaim *'ahhh'*, *'oooh'* and *'uhhh'* on your exhale.
- Observe the different amount of breath and energy used in both exercises

Breathing with a Bang

- Start with your hands over your heart
- Take a deep breath in as you raise your hands over your head
- Clap your hands - BANG!
- Exhale, lowering your hands to your lap

Puffy Cheeks

- Take a deep breath in, puff out your cheeks and push the air through your lips as you exhale making a quiet *'prrrrrr'* noise (unvoiced)

Lip Rolls

- Take a deep breath in, relax your lips and blow a stream of air through them making a *'brrr'* sound (voiced). Your lips will vibrate against each other and tickle!
- You can do this exercise again adding a siren sound around the choir

Tongue Rolls

- Take a deep breath in and let your tongue make rapid movements in your mouth (roll your tongue) making a *'rrrr'* sound.

DIAPHRAGM EXERCISES

Motorbike Race

- Split the choir in two groups. One groups pretends they are riding drive a heavy Harley Davidson motorbike, the other group has got a small motor scooter, or vesper.

- Pretend both groups are waiting at a red traffic light

- Each revs up their engine, a little bit at first, than louder and louder. As the light turns orange... then green.... and they are off!!

Snake Breathing

- Take an in breath and push little hisses out until you run out of breath

Birthday

- Inhale with your hands on your rib cage and fill your lungs

- Imagine blowing out six individual birthday candles

- Repeat with eight candles

Twice as fast

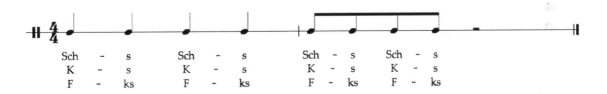

All Aboard!

- Imagine you are a steam locomotive: *'chooga, chooga, chooga'*

- Start slowly, then speed up the train and add a whistle!

Row the boat

- Speak the rhythm of 'Row row row your boat' on a *'k'* sound

- Divide the choir into 3 groups and do as a round with each group using a different consonant *'p'*, *'t'* and *'f'*

Repeat with various well-known rounds such as 'London's Burning', 'Frère Jacques' etc.

Engine Room

- Accenting the consonants, rhythmically speak the base rhythm *'Sss - Sch - Fff - (rest)'*

- Build your own 'engine room' splitting the choir to groups and using different consonant sounds and layering rhythms, for example:

  - 'Money - money - money - money' in double time to *'Sss - Sch - Fff - (rest)'*

  - Swing rhythm *'S - s's - S - s's - S - s's - S'* etc.

Out of Puff

- Accent the consonants and rhythms on these silly sayings
  - Piff-puff-puff
  - Kitty-kitty-kitty-cat
  - Pitter-patter-pitterpat
  - Ziggezagezigge zagge hoi hoi hoi
  - Zoo ma zoo ma zoo ma ma

Kicking Consonants

- Accent the consonants and rhythms (also use words from the repertoire the choir is learning)
  - *T T T T* Tiger
  - *K K K K* Kettle
  - *P P P P* Pony
  - *F F F F* Fire
  - *Sch Sch Sch Sch* Schamen
  - *S S S S* Snake
  - *K K K K* King
  - *T T T T* Toast
  - *F F F F* Fight
  - *S S S S* Snow

Dog's Dinner

- Pant for 30 seconds like a dog after a good run

- Bark like a big Rottweiler, then like a medium sized Terrier and finally like a little Chihuahua

Spirit of Vitality

- Imagine you are a Karate fighter and about to chop through some bricks with your bare hand

- Take a deep breath, gather your energy and exhale with a chopping movement exclaiming *'Ha'*!

Santa Claus

- Imagine you are Santa Claus and you greet the children with a hearty *'ho ho ho ho ho'*. Make sure you can feel your diaphragm move!

- Do the same pretending to be a silly schoolgirl giggling *'hee hee hee hee hee!'*

Monkeys!

- Say the following, pushing each syllable from the diaphragm (repeat)
  - *'yu - ho - ha - hey - hee'*

Football Chant

- Chant the following rhythm together on a *'k'*

- Now split the choir into three groups
  - The first group says this rhythm on a *'k'*
  - The second group enters after beat 1 on a *'t'*
  - The third groups enters after beat 1 of the second group on a *'p'*

Drum Kit

- Split the choir into three groups and build your drum kit from the bass drum up to the hi-hat. A great way to introduce or support any swing tune!

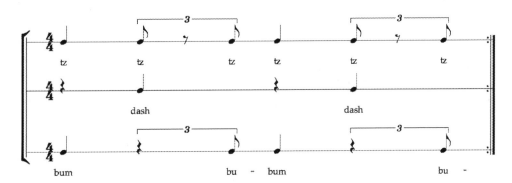

CHAPTER 3

ARTICULATION

DICTION

PRINCIPLES

Singing is essentially storytelling with music, therefore it is crucial that the audience should clearly understand the words that are sung.

Diction comprises pronunciation, enunciation and articulation of words. A well-known tongue twister states that 'Diction is done with the tip of the tongue', however, many more parts of the mouth are involved, especially the teeth and lips.

In singing, articulation differs from spoken words in that the singer aims to hold on to vowel sounds as much as possible as they carry sound, whereas consonants are used to separate words and punctuate lyrics.

All vowel sounds in the English language are used in the sentence below, roughly going anti-clockwise around the outside of the IPA vowel diagram.

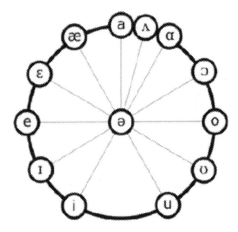

"Who would know aught of art must learn and take his ease"

All of these sounds are placed and resonate in different parts of the mouth. By taking a big yawn you can get an idea of the placement.

In order to create a unified blend within the choir, the singers need to create the same vowel shapes for a cohesive sound.

PREPARATORY EXERCISES

In order to get crisp diction, articulation and pronunciation need to be slightly exaggerated. This requires movement of the jaw.

1. Find the place where your jaw is hinged to your skull, just below your cheekbones. Massage this point. Release the tension there. Have a good yawn.

2. Pretend that you are chewing some gum

3. Pretend to chew a big piece of steak. Then some carrot sticks. Munch on some tiny pretzels.

4. Big Face Little Face: Purse your lips as if you want to give someone a little kiss and then open your mouth wide like a roaring tiger

5. Stick out your tongue like a naughty child. Pull it back as far as possible.

6. Move your tongue around the outside of your mouth as if licking some delicious ice cream off your face.

7. Open your mouth slightly and make a fast 'llllllllll' sound with your tongue going up and down touching your lips and then from left to right (voiced).

8. Get a champagne cork and put it between your teeth. Say any tongue twister or lyric three times with the cork between your teeth. Remove the cork and repeat. You will notice a much crisper and clearer pronunciation!

Tongue Twister Practice Tips

The purpose of practicing tongue twisters is to achieve excellent articulation.

1. Start at a slow tempo and only increase the speed when the diction is crystal clear

2. Ask the choir members to bring along a small mirror. Demonstrate the mouth shapes for the exercises and let the singers look into their mirrors to see if they are copying it correctly.

3. If the repertoire poses some challenging lyrics use those as tongue twisters

4. Start easy and then choose more lyrically and melodically challenging tongue twisters as you progress

5. At this stage of the warm up we're focusing on articulation rather than melody so you can simply sing up four notes and then down again to your starting note (see the melody under 'Short & Sweet'), moving up a semi-tone for each new tongue twister.

6. The toung twisters become more challenging lyrically and also melodically as we progress.

TONGUE TWISTERS

I like my bike I like my bike I like my bike I like my bike

I like my bike I like my bike I like my bike......

Short & Sweet

- I like my bike
- Short sleeved shirts (triplet quaver rhythm)
- Top chopstick shops
- Unique New York
- Stupid superstition (five quaver rhythm)
- World wide web
- Spectacular spectacles (seven quaver rhythm)
- A Swiss wrist watch
- Truly rural

Numbers

- One wandering worm
- Two tickets to Tooting
- Three thick things
- Four furious friends
- Five forgetful French men
- Six crisp snacks
- Seven sizzling sausages
- Eight grey geese
- Nine nosey nuns
- Ten tired tigers

Posh!

- The tip of the tongue, the teeth and the lips
- Diction is done with the tip of the tongue
- Lucy likes light literature
- Nine nimble noblemen nibbled nuts
- The rain in Spain falls mainly on the plane
- Fine white vinegar with veal
- Proper copper coffee pot

Amazing Alliteration

- Double bubble gum bubbles double
- Tom stops Ron's long song
- Oily Ollie oils oily autos
- Mallory's hourly salary

On Stage

- Paul, please pause for proper applause
- Thelma sings the theme song
- A laurel crowned clown
- Carla cued Clive's curtain call
- Aging actors earned accolade

Holy Moses!

- No roses grow on Moses nose
- Sarah sang some sacred songs
- Peter posted precious presents
- Luke listens to Latin liturgies
- Particular stickers attract active vicars

Fishy!

- Clean clams crammed in clean cans
- For fine fresh fish phone Phil
- Try fat flat flounders
- Francis fries fresh fish filets
- No shark shares swordfish steak

Christmas

- Seven Santa's sang silly songs.
- Tiny Timmy trims the tree with tinsel.
- Bobby brings bright bells.
- Rudolph runs rings 'round Rover
- Eleven elves ate everything
- Carol comes to the Christmas carol concert

'R's'

- Red lorry, yellow lorry
- A real weird rear wheel
- Rubber baby buggy bumpers
- Ripples in the rock pool, ripples in the sea
- Rolling red wagons

'Th's'

- Mr. Smith's fish sauce shop
- The Leith police dismisses dismisseth us
- Three free throws
- Six thick thistle sticks
- Red leather, yellow leather

Summer

- Surely the sun shall shine soon
- Some shun summer sunshine
- Choosing tulips during June

Ship Ahoy!

- A cheap ship trip
- Diving dolphins dined on doughnuts
- Sure the ship's shipshape, sir
- Seven silver seals sitting in the sun
- Fran feeds fish fresh fish food
- The shallow ship showed signs of sinking

Learning Language

- Assonance is asking Hannah, have you had the last of that banana?
- Alliteration loves licking lollies, likes laughing loudly, leaves Leo lonely
- Assonance is singing shrilly; stick this pin in Lillie's pig. It thinks it's silly
- Alliteration breeds bouncing babies, bowls balls badly, brings Barry biscuits/

by kind permission of Sharon Durant

It's Complicated!

- Aristotle lost his bottle when he spied and axolotl
- Which wristwatch is a Swiss wristwatch?
- The theory of relativity is nonsensical to traditional mathematicians
- Strange strategic statistics
- Octopi occupy a porcupine's mind
- Zoologists illogically love to read astrology

Going Round in Circles

- Round and round the rugged rock the ragged rascal ran
- Aristotle lost his bottle when he spied an axolotl
- Fancy Nancy didn't fancy doing fancy work
- You can play the ukulele, you can play it well

Another and Another

- Another and another and another...
- Forever and forever and forever...
- Together and together and together...

These tongue twisters can also be sung in counter motion or as a round with the second group starting when the first group sing the third note.

Smelly

- Steven sells smelly socks
- Freshly fried flying fish
- Lisa laughs listlessly
- Spread it thick say it quick
- Harry knew 'you know who'

Confusing

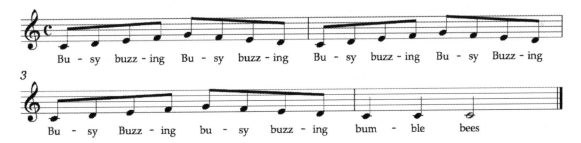

- Busy buzzing, busy buzzing (1), busy buzzing, busy buzzing (2), buzy buzzing, buzy buzzing (3) bumble bees
- Double bubble (x3)...bubble gum
- Proper copper (x3)...coffee pot
- Little ladies' (x3)...lentil soup
- Truly rural (x3)...holidays

Spooky!

- He thrusts his fist against a post and still insists he sees a ghost
- There was a little witch which switched from Chester over to Ipswich
- A pretty pack of pesky pixies picked a pot of pickled peas
- Yoda met a Yeti on the Plains of Serengeti

EDIBLE TONGUE TWISTERS

An Italian Meal

An-ti pas-ti An-ti pas-ti An-ti pas-ti An-ti pas-ti An-ti pas-ti An-ti pas-ti An-ti pas-ti

- Antipasti, Tagliatele, Fettuccine, Carbonara, Mozzarella, Panettone, un Espresso!

An Indian Meal

Chick en ti-kka Chick en ti-kka Chick en ti-kka start-er with nan and pi-lau rice

- Chicken Tikka, Chicken Tikka, Chicken Tikka starter with Nan and Pilau rice
- Chicken Tikka, Mango Chutney and a Pint of Lager with Nan and Pilau rice

British Fare

Che-shire Chut-ney Che-shire Chut-ney   Che-shire Chut-ney   Che-shire Chut-ney

3

Che-shire Chut-ney Che-shire Chut-ney   Che-shire Chut-ney –

- Cheshire chutney, Cheshire chutney
- Mersey munchies, Mersey munchies
- Wiltshire warthog, Wiltshire warthog
- Sussex sausages, Sussex sausages
- Berkshire burgers, Berkshire burgers

Texmex

- Chuck a chop of chicken, Or chop a chipotle chilli up!

TEAM TONGUE TWISTERS

Diddly dee, diddly dee, diddly diddly diddly dee!

This exercise helps to get the group focused and on task.

Establish a rhythm. Each person says one word round the circle, keeping to the rhythm. At the end of a sequence, whoever is next starts the sequence with another first letter, for example,

- Middly mee, middly mee, middly middly middly mee
- Tiddly tee, tiddly tee, tiddly tiddly tiddly tee etc.
- Fiddely fee...

What's in a Name?

This is a great ice-breaker for the choir. Ask each person to make up a tongue twister about their neighbour to the right or left and then use these as warm-ups in your rehearsals. This will help people to get to know each other's names as well as practicing articulation and pronunciation!

Examples might include:

- Linda loves lovely lullabies
- June juggles jigsaw puzzles
- Lonnie loves luxury lollipops
- Steph sails seven seas
- Tina teachers terrible tongue twisters
- Jon jams gentle jazz
- Mags makes many macaroons
- Sheila sells shimmering starfish

These steps might help to come up with some good ones:

- Say your choir partners first name
- Choose a verb and a noun, ideally starting with the same letter as their name - what did they do to what?
- Say where all this took place!

For example, Tina teaches Tango in Thailand!

Tina Reibl

TONGUE TWISTER POEMS

All the poems below are spoken. Teach the choir two lines at a time. If you're feeling adventurous you can try adding some brain gym exercises to the poems too!

Warming Up

Warming up and warming down is worth a little time
Much can be accomplished with some rhythm and some rhyme
They will help your voice to get itself to maxi-range
Even though the sounds of each may be a little strange

Super Californian Surfers

Supercaliforniasurfers experts on the ocean,
Even though the sums of them do not wear suntan lotion
But when they hit the waves real hard they're always in the motion,
Supercaliforniasurfers experts on the ocean

(What famous tune could this also be sung to?)

Washerwoman

In the deep, dark jungle where nobody goes,
There's a wishy-washy washerwoman washing her clothes.
She goes "Ooh, ahh, ooh, ahh, Ooh ahh ahh"

Wishy Washy Washer Woman Wishy Washy Washer Woman
Wishy Washy Washer Woman Wishy Washy Washer Woman

In the deep, dark jungle where nobody goes,
There's a wishy-washy washerwoman smelling a rose.
She goes "smell –ah! Smell -ah!"

Wishy Washy Washer Woman Wishy Washy Washer Woman
Wishy Washy Washer Woman Wishy Washy Washer Woman

Hope

Who hath not learned, in hours of faith,
The truth to flesh and sense unknown,
That Life is ever lord of Death,
And Love can never lose its' own!

John Greenleaf Whittier

Encouragement

"Will you walk a little faster?" said a whiting to the snail,
"There's a porpoise close behind us and he's treading on my tail.
See how eagerly the lobsters and the turtles all advance!
They are waiting on the shingle - will you come and join the dance?
Will you, won't you, will you, won't you, will you join the dance?
Won't you, will you, won't you, will you, won't you join the dance?"

Lewis Caroll

Fisher's Fish

There was a fisherman named Fisher
who fished for some fish in a fissure.
Till a fish with a grin,
pulled the fisherman in.
Now they're fishing the fissure for Fisher.

A Bear Tale

I cannot bear to see a bear
Bear down upon a hare.
When bare of hair he strips the hare,
Right there I cry, "Forbear'
Centipede's Confusion

A centipede was happy quite until a frog in fun said 'Pray, which leg comes after
which'? This raised her mind to such a pitch, she lay distracted in a ditch, considering
how to run!

Katherine Craster

A Smelly Story

A skunk sat on a stump.
The skunk thought the stump stunk.
The stump thought the skunk stunk.
No Choice
Whether the weather be cold,
or whether the weather be hot.
We'll whether together, whatever the weather,
whether we like it or not.

John Ruskin

Wedding Vows

A certain young fellow named Beebee
Wished to marry a lady named Phoebe
"But," he said. "I must see
What the minister's fee be
Before Phoebe be Phoebe Beebee"

Edward Lear

Sad Ending

To sit in solemn silence on a dull, dark dock,
In a pestilential prison, with a life-long lock,
Awaiting the sensation of a short, sharp shock,
From a cheap and chippy chopper on a big black block!

W. S. Gilbert

TONGUE TWISTER QUODLIBETS

Superimposing tongue twisters on top of each other is great fun and a wonderful exercise in keeping rhythm. After learning each one and putting them together you can ask the choir to:

- Swap parts on a hand signal you give them
- Clap the rhythm
- Drop in and out on a signal you give them

Reindeer in the Kitchen!

- How many deer would a reindeer reign if a reindeer could reign deer?
- Left, left, I left my jar of Branston Pickle, right, right, right on the bottom of the kitchen floor

Here the choir stamps on the pulse. For the 'Branston Pickle' tongue twister the left or right leg leads when as the words are being said.

Woodchuckers Cheque

- How much wood would a woodchuck chuck if a woodchuck could chuck wood?
- You know I've got a cheque in the bag, you know I've got a cheque. You know I've got a cheque in the bag, check!

Ice Cold

- How many boards could the Mongols hoard if the Mongol hordes got bored?
- I scream, you scream, we all scream for ice cream!

Poor Bear

- The big black bug bit the big black bear, made the big black bear bleed blood
- How many saws could a see-saw saw, if a see-saw could saw saws?

Japanese Choral

Give different pitches and speak the following rhythms of Japanese car names

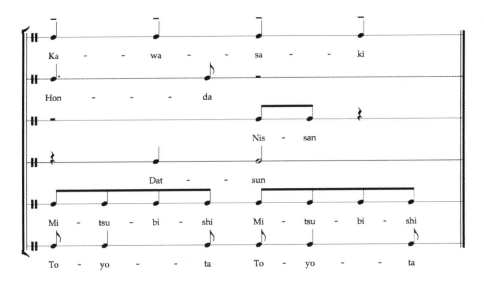

You can build a vocal symphony by adding or removing more parts.

Japanese Choral

This can also be done with musical terms which are spoken depicting their meaning e.g.

- Piano (spoken softly)
- Fortissimo (spoken loudly)
- Crescendo (getting louder)
- Diminuendo (getting quieter)
- Presto (spoken quickly)
- Largo (spoken slowly) etc.

ROBIN HOOD VARIATIONS

Most people will know the 'Robin Hood' tune from the William Tell Overture. So you can have a bit of fun with it using different variations.

With the following variations you can:

1. Indicate if you want it sung presto, largo, espressivo, forte, pianissimo etc.

2. Request different singing styles:

   – Like you've just won the lottery

   – Like you are a holy person giving someone a blessing

   – Like an angry teenager complaining

Robin Hood

- Robin Hood, Robin Hood, Robin Hood Hood Hood...

- Merry Men...

- Friar Tuck...

- Little John...

- Nottingham...

- Marian...

Orders!

- Bite A Bun, Bite A Bun, Bite A Bun, Bun, Bun...

- Wear a wig...

- Touch your toes...

- Sing a song...

- Try a trick...

- Run around...

- Shoot a shark...

- Fry a fish...

- Catch a cold...

Comes in all Sizes

- Minimum, minimum, minimum, mum, mum... (piano)

- Medium... (mezzo piano)

- Maximum... (forte)

Complete Nonsense

- Papa's got a head like a ping pong ball, Papa's got a head like a ping pong ball, Papa's got a head like a ping pong ball, just like a ping pong ball!

- Mama's got a head like a ming mong mall...

- Granny's got a head like a ging gong gall...

- Nana's got a head like a ning nong nall...

The Ping Pong Overture

Split the choir into two groups and learn the parts for Voice A and Voice B. Sing through with two verses with each group swapping parts.

Rossini

LIMERICKS

There was an Old Man in a tree,
Who was horribly bored by a bee.
When they said "Does it buzz?"
He replied "Yes, it does!
It's a regular brute of a bee!"
—*Edward Lear*

There was a Young Lady whose chin
Resembled the point of a pin:
So she had it made sharp,
And purchased a harp,
And played several tunes with her chin.
—*Edward Lear*

There was an old woman of Bath
And she was as thin as a lath
She was as brown as a berry
With a nose like a cherry
This skinny old woman of Bath
—*John Harris*

'Tis strange how the newspapers honour
A creature that's called Prima Donna
They say not a thing
Of how she can sing
But reams of the clothes she has on her.
—*Eugene Field*

You can create your own Limericks on https://www.poem-generator.org.uk

CHAPTER 4

THE REHEARSAL

THE NON-AUDITIONED CHOIR

'Since singing is so good a thing, I wish all men would learn to sing' said William Byrd in 1588 and many people are now following his wish. Indeed, there is much research to support this – from psychological well-being to music therapy and from cardiology to the classroom.

There are an increasing number of choirs; including community choirs, rock choirs, junior or senior choirs and workplace choirs, which are non-auditioned, inclusive and a fun place to sing.

As many of the members will not know how to read music it is essential to build aural and musicianship skills as well as aiming for a good quality of sound and blend.

Teaching songs will probably follow the oral tradition and use call and response patterns, teaching by rote and repetition.

Choristers should also learn

- Good posture
- Good breathing and articulation
- Creating a beautiful tone
- Concentrating for extended periods of time
- Connecting with the other members of the choir

Rehearsals ought to have a clear structure and not be too long and a variety of challenges will keep the interest up.

Silence should be the framework for all activities, always start from silence and internal focus.

An achievable and enjoyable repertoire will help the choir to sing with confidence and gain a sense of achievement.

THE ELEMENTS OF A GOOD REHEARSAL

Announcements

Announcements should be kept brief and clear. If you want choristers to remember what you said follow the old rule: 'tell them what you will tell them, tell them, tell them what you told them'!

Warm up

The warm-up does not necessarily have to be related to the main body of rehearsal, however if there are difficult passages of lyrics or breathing challenges you should of course use those in your actual warm-up.

Musicianship training should be always in the conductors mind. The warm ups provide ample opportunities to practice dynamics, how to follow conductors gestures, good posture and facial expression, listening to each other and creating unified vowel sounds.

An ideal rehearsal would look like this:

Total rehearsal time	60 minutes	90 minutes
Announcements	5 minutes	5 minutes
Warm-up	10 minutes	15 minutes
Aural work	5 minutes	5 minutes
Warm-up song e.g. a round	10 minutes	10 minutes
Main music practice	30 minutes	55 minutes

THE AUDITIONED CHOIR

Most choirs coming from the classic/church music tradition are auditioned, aiming to sing soprano, alto, tenor, bass (SATB) literature with a lovely tone, balance and expression.

In addition, singers should learn

- To own the music they are singing
- To think creatively
- To read music

There should be high expectations of punctuality, engagement, achievement and commitment.

Whether it is a gospel or madrigal choir, the choir practice should still provide an opportunity for more advanced aural work. This will help singers to pitch more confidently and sight-read with more ease.

Aural work and sight-reading can be an integral part of the music practice in a choir that is able to sight at sight. Separating out and clapping or speaking complicated rhythms, looking at intervals in difficult passages is common practice in the majority of choirs anyway.

An ideal rehearsal would look like this:

Total rehearsal time	60 minutes	90 minutes	120 minutes
Announcements	5 minutes	5 minutes	5 minutes
Warm-up	10 minutes	15 minutes	15 minutes
Aural work	5 minutes	5 minutes	10 minutes
Sight reading	10 minutes	5 minutes	10 minutes
Main music practice	30 minutes	55 minutes	70 minutes
Break	N/a	5 minute comfort break	10 minutes

If the rehearsal is a long one it is helpful to put a quick energiser after the break to get singers re-focused.

REHEARSAL PLAN

Date:

Announcements

Warm-ups

Body-warm up

Breathing exercises

Tongue twisters

Vocal exercises

Technical focus

Warm-up song

Repertoire New

Repertoire Old

Goals Tonight

A good choir session will give the choristers a wonderful uplift. Having exercised their body, minds and vocal folds (cords), and created harmony, they will take home a feeling of well-being and joy. It doesn't get much better than that!

To finish with another quote:

"I don't sing because I'm happy, I'm happy because I sing."

William James

APPENDIX

Resources

Vocal Exercises to use in Choral Setting:

Warm-Ups for Pop, Jazz and Show Choirs	Kirby Shaw Hal Leonard Publishing
Funky 'n Fun	Kim Chandler http://www.funkynfun.com
Voice Builders for Better Choirs	Emily Crocker Hal Leonard Publishing
Ultimate Vocal Voyage	Daniel Zangger Borch Notfabriken Publishing
The Complete Choral Warm-Up Book	Robinson/Althouse Alfred Choral Builders
Stimmicals 1	Uli Fuehre, Fidula Publishing

Warm-ups:

Jetse Bremer http://www.jetsebremer.nl/en

On Choral Leadership/Conducting:

The Contemporary Chorus Alfred Publishing	Carl Strommen,
The Perfect Blend Shawnee Press Vocal Library	Timothy Seelig,

Song Collections:

The whole 'Singing for Pleasure' Book set available at:
http://www.singforpleasure.org.uk/shop

Popular Voiceworks 1 & 2	Charles Beale and Steve Milloy,

About The Author

Tina Reibl has worked as an enthusiastic vocal teacher, musical animator and workshop leader for 25 years.

After obtaining a Postgraduate Degree from the Guildhall School in London, she briefly was a professional singer before pursuing her real passion for education.

Tina's teaching career took her from working as a peripatetic singing teacher to lecturing Performing Arts at College followed by a role as teacher of Musical Theatre at a well-known stage school.

After working as an educational consultant Tina has travelled throughout the UK as a Teacher's Trainer since 2006, both for leading private training companies and Trinity College London specializing in accelerated learning and vocal and choral training courses.

As well as running Maidenheads' large Community Choir she is working internationally on cruise ships as a choir mistress and offers singing retreats around the world.

Tina's music sessions are invariably cheerful, energetic, inspirational and enjoyable. She describes herself as a 'edutainer'.

Printed in the United States
By Bookmasters